MAD LIBS®

GROSS ME OUT
MAD LIBS

by Gabriella DeGennaro

MAD LIBS
An imprint of Penguin Random House LLC, New York

First published in the United States of America by Mad Libs,
an imprint of Penguin Random House LLC, New York, 2023

Mad Libs format and text copyright © 2023 by Penguin Random House LLC

Concept created by Roger Price & Leonard Stern

Cover illustration by Scott Brooks

Visit us online at penguinrandomhouse.com.

Printed in the United States of America

ISBN 9780593658369
3 5 7 9 10 8 6 4
COMR

MAD LIBS

INSTRUCTIONS

MAD LIBS® is a game for people who don't like games!
It can be played by one, two, three, four, or forty.

• RIDICULOUSLY SIMPLE DIRECTIONS

In this tablet you will find stories containing blank spaces where words
are left out. One player, the READER, selects one of these stories. The
READER does not tell anyone what the story is about. Instead, he/she asks
the other players, the WRITERS, to give him/her words. These words are
used to fill in the blank spaces in the story.

• TO PLAY

The READER asks each WRITER in turn to call out a word—an adjective or
a noun or whatever the space calls for—and uses them to fill in the blank
spaces in the story. The result is a MAD LIBS® game.

When the READER then reads the completed MAD LIBS® game to the other
players, they will discover that they have written a story that is fantastic,
screamingly funny, shocking, silly, crazy, or just plain dumb—depending
upon which words each WRITER called out.

• EXAMPLE (*Before* and *After*)

"_____!" he said _____
                EXCLAMATION   ADVERB

as he jumped into his convertible _____ and
                                            NOUN

drove off with his _____ wife.
                            ADJECTIVE

"_____OUCH_____!" he said _____HAPPILY_____
                EXCLAMATION   ADVERB

as he jumped into his convertible _____CAT_____ and
                                            NOUN

drove off with his _____BRAVE_____ wife.
                            ADJECTIVE

MAD LIBS

QUICK REVIEW

In case you have forgotten what adjectives, adverbs, nouns, and verbs are, here is a quick review:

An ADJECTIVE describes something or somebody. *Lumpy*, *soft*, *ugly*, *messy*, and *short* are adjectives.

An ADVERB tells how something is done. It modifies a verb and usually ends in "ly." *Modestly*, *stupidly*, *greedily*, and *carefully* are adverbs.

A NOUN is the name of a person, place, or thing. *Sidewalk*, *umbrella*, *bridle*, *bathtub*, and *nose* are nouns.

A VERB is an action word. *Run*, *pitch*, *jump*, and *swim* are verbs. Put the verbs in past tense if the directions say PAST TENSE. *Ran*, *pitched*, *jumped*, and *swam* are verbs in the past tense.

When we ask for A PLACE, we mean any sort of place: a country or city (*Spain*, *Cleveland*) or a room (*bathroom*, *kitchen*).

An EXCLAMATION or SILLY WORD is any sort of funny sound, gasp, grunt, or outcry, like *Wow!*, *Ouch!*, *Whomp!*, *Ick!*, and *Gadzooks!*

When we ask for specific words, like a NUMBER, a COLOR, an ANIMAL, or a PART OF THE BODY, we mean a word that is one of those things, like *seven*, *blue*, *horse*, or *head*.

When we ask for a PLURAL, it means more than one. For example, *cat* pluralized is *cats*.

MAD LIBS® is fun to play with friends, but you can also play it by yourself! To begin with, DO NOT look at the story on the page below. Fill in the blanks on this page with the words called for. Then, using the words you have selected, fill in the blank spaces in the story.

Now you've created your own hilarious MAD LIBS® game!

GET GROSS GUIDE

ADJECTIVE _____

VERB _____

NOUN _____

PART OF THE BODY _____

ADJECTIVE _____

NOUN _____

VERB ENDING IN "ING" _____

NOUN _____

ANIMAL _____

PART OF THE BODY _____

TYPE OF FOOD _____

VERB _____

VEHICLE _____

VERB _____

VERB _____

PART OF THE BODY (PLURAL) _____

ARTICLE OF CLOTHING _____

MAD LIBS®

GET GROSS GUIDE

How _____blue_____ (ADJECTIVE) can you get? _____Bootyshake_____ (VERB) your _____potato salad_____ (NOUN) -scented deodorant goodbye, toss your _____tailbone_____ (PART OF THE BODY) -brush in the trash, and follow these steps for extreme grossness:

1. Build up some _____slimy_____ (ADJECTIVE) B-O! When you get home from _____toilet_____ (NOUN) practice or _____sitting_____ (VERB ENDING IN "ING") outside, skip showering! Who needs a loofah and _____popcorn_____ (NOUN) -berry bubble bath? Not you!

2. Chew your food like a/an _____skunk_____ (ANIMAL) . . . with your _____wrist_____ (PART OF THE BODY) wide open! Send chunks of _____cheese burger_____ (TYPE OF FOOD) flying with every bite! And don't forget to _____jump_____ (VERB) and chew at the same time!

3. Got gas? Save it for the next _____lamburini_____ (VEHICLE) ride on your way to school! Roll the windows up and _____talking_____ (VERB)!

4. Step in gum? _____Peeing_____ (VERB) it! Use your _____hands_____ (PART OF THE BODY (PLURAL)) to remove it from your _____Nikes_____ (ARTICLE OF CLOTHING) and chew!

MAD LIBS® is fun to play with friends, but you can also play it by yourself! To begin with, DO NOT look at the story on the page below. Fill in the blanks on this page with the words called for. Then, using the words you have selected, fill in the blank spaces in the story.

Now you've created your own hilarious MAD LIBS® game!

DOUBLE-DOG DARE

FIRST NAME _____

CELEBRITY _____

ADJECTIVE _____

TYPE OF CONTAINER _____

NOUN _____

SAME CELEBRITY _____

VERB _____

SAME CELEBRITY _____

ADJECTIVE _____

ANIMAL _____

SAME CELEBRITY _____

ADJECTIVE _____

EXCLAMATION _____

VERB (PAST TENSE) _____

SAME CELEBRITY _____

PERSON YOU KNOW _____

SAME FIRST NAME _____

VERB ENDING IN "ING" _____

MAD LIBS®

DOUBLE-DOG DARE

__Ms. Rtato__ and his little brother __theroke__ were
FIRST NAME   CELEBRITY

cleaning out the fridge, the last chore on Mom's list, when they both

spotted something green and ___tolot___ dripping out of a/an
                              ADJECTIVE

___cool ase___. Could it be Grandpa's ___te ing___ loaf? They
TYPE OF CONTAINER   NOUN

hadn't had that for dinner in months! ___tho rot___ was throwing it
                                        SAME CELEBRITY

away when his big brother stopped him. "I dare you to ___tiny___
                                                       VERB

it," he said. ___Vock___ refused—he couldn't eat that
              SAME CELEBRITY

_____ thing! It was covered in mold! But his older brother
ADJECTIVE

wouldn't take no for an answer. "I double-_____ dare you,"
                                          ANIMAL

he said. ___laas___ froze. He couldn't turn down that kind of
         SAME CELEBRITY

dare! So, he prepared to do the unthinkable. He took a good look at the

___Bate___, slimy food, ready to take a bite, and . . . ___cod___!
ADJECTIVE   EXCLAMATION

He ___saton___ all over the kitchen floor. ___rocke___
   VERB (PAST TENSE)   SAME CELEBRITY

ran off, crying to ___tolot Ezra___. And ___Ezra___, well, he
                   PERSON YOU KNOW   SAME FIRST NAME

had to do one more chore for Mom . . . ___kikin___
                                        VERB ENDING IN "ING"

the kitchen floor!

MAD LIBS® is fun to play with friends, but you can also play it by yourself! To begin with, DO NOT look at the story on the page below. Fill in the blanks on this page with the words called for. Then, using the words you have selected, fill in the blank spaces in the story.

Now you've created your own hilarious MAD LIBS® game!

HISTORY STINKS!

VERB ENDING IN "ING" _____

ADJECTIVE _____

ANIMAL _____

ADJECTIVE _____

NOUN _____

NOUN _____

ADJECTIVE _____

A PLACE _____

TYPE OF BUILDING (PLURAL) _____

NUMBER _____

ADJECTIVE _____

COUNTRY _____

ADVERB _____

LAST NAME _____

PLURAL NOUN _____

ANIMAL _____

PLURAL NOUN _____

MAD LIBS®

HISTORY STINKS!

Have fun ___resling___ these historical facts:
VERB ENDING IN "ING"

1. In ___Dosk___ folk medicine, fresh ___elfint___ dung was
   ADJECTIVE   ANIMAL
   used to cure a/an ___iotwb___ nose.
                      ADJECTIVE

2. Instead of ___sisr s___ paper, ancient Romans used a sponge
              NOUN
   attached to a/an _____ to clean themselves. And then
                        NOUN
   they shared it!

3. Speaking of the _____ Romans, privacy in (the)
                        ADJECTIVE
   _____ was unlikely. Public _____ had
        A PLACE   TYPE OF BUILDING (PLURAL)
   "toilets" that were only _____ inches apart!
                               NUMBER

4. The " _____ Stink" of 1858 in London, _____,
            ADJECTIVE   COUNTRY
   was a/an _____ hot summer when the River _____
             ADVERB   LAST NAME
   stunk up the city with the smell of _____.
                                         PLURAL NOUN

5. What happens if you time travel to ancient Egypt and you
   have forgotten your toothpaste? Borrow someone else's made
   from powdered _____ hooves, eggshells, and
                       ANIMAL
   _____!
        PLURAL NOUN

MAD LIBS® is fun to play with friends, but you can also play it by yourself! To begin with, DO NOT look at the story on the page below. Fill in the blanks on this page with the words called for. Then, using the words you have selected, fill in the blank spaces in the story.

Now you've created your own hilarious MAD LIBS® game!

FAIRY GROSS-MOTHER

VERB ENDING IN "ING" _____

NOUN _____

YOUR NAME _____

NOUN _____

PLURAL NOUN _____

ADVERB _____

VERB _____

PART OF THE BODY _____

TYPE OF LIQUID _____

ADJECTIVE _____

VERB _____

ADVERB _____

ANIMAL _____

NUMBER _____

PART OF THE BODY _____

NUMBER _____

VERB _____

PLURAL NOUN _____

MAD LIBS®

FAIRY GROSS-MOTHER

Have you ever wondered what happens if you sneeze while

_____ on a shooting _____? Spoiler alert: It's
VERB ENDING IN "ING"   NOUN

how I got stuck with _____, my fairy *gross*-mother. Real
                                       YOUR NAME

fairy _____-mothers turn homework into cuddly _____,
            NOUN   PLURAL NOUN

make bedrooms _____ clean, and can _____
                       ADVERB   VERB

cookies with the flick of a wand! My fairy gross-mother, on the other

_____, only knows how to make mud _____-shakes
PART OF THE BODY   TYPE OF LIQUID

and turns my room into a/an _____ swamp! I have to
                                  ADJECTIVE

_____ myself from making wishes because they all turn
             VERB

out _____·_____! Like the time I wished for a cute baby
                ADVERB

_____ and got a/an _____-headed toad instead! Or
  ANIMAL   NUMBER

when I wished for my pimple to go away before picture day, and she

covered my _____ with _____ more! Sometimes, I
         PART OF THE BODY   NUMBER

just want to _____, "I wish she would go away!" But I think
             VERB

that would just make it worse . . . Uh-oh! I said "I wish." And she heard

me! My room is filling up with slugs and _____. This can't
                                   PLURAL NOUN

be good . . .

MAD LIBS® is fun to play with friends, but you can also play it by yourself! To begin with, DO NOT look at the story on the page below. Fill in the blanks on this page with the words called for. Then, using the words you have selected, fill in the blank spaces in the story.

Now you've created your own hilarious MAD LIBS® game!

HOW NASTY?

NUMBER _____

ADJECTIVE _____

VERB ENDING IN "ING" _____

TYPE OF FOOD (PLURAL) _____

ARTICLE OF CLOTHING _____

NOUN _____

ANIMAL _____

NUMBER _____

NOUN _____

LETTER OF THE ALPHABET _____

ADJECTIVE _____

TYPE OF CONTAINER _____

NOUN _____

PART OF THE BODY _____

TYPE OF LIQUID _____

ADJECTIVE _____

NOUN _____

MAD LIBS®

HOW NASTY?

On a scale of one to _____, with ten being the nastiest, rate
                        NUMBER

these _____ scenarios:
          ADJECTIVE

1. Dumpster _____ through huge piles of rotten
                  VERB ENDING IN "ING"

   _____ wearing only a tropical-print bathing
     TYPE OF FOOD (PLURAL)

   _____. Nasty Rating: __
     ARTICLE OF CLOTHING

2. Sharing a melting _____-cream cone with your pet
                          NOUN

   _____. Nasty Rating: __
      ANIMAL

3. Watching _____ hours of _____-popping videos
                NUMBER   NOUN

   on _____-Tube. Nasty Rating: __
      LETTER OF THE ALPHABET

4. Collecting _____ toenails in a/an _____.
                  ADJECTIVE   TYPE OF CONTAINER

   Nasty Rating: __

5. Finding a used _____-Aid stuck to your _____
                      NOUN   PART OF THE BODY

   after swimming at the water park. Nasty Rating: __

6. Dunking your retainer into _____ before wearing it.
                                  TYPE OF LIQUID

   Nasty Rating: __

7. Finding a/an _____ hair on your _____ nuggets
                    ADJECTIVE   NOUN

   but eating them anyway. Nasty Rating: __

MAD LIBS® is fun to play with friends, but you can also play it by yourself! To begin with, DO NOT look at the story on the page below. Fill in the blanks on this page with the words called for. Then, using the words you have selected, fill in the blank spaces in the story.

Now you've created your own hilarious MAD LIBS® game!

WHO TOOTED?

PLURAL NOUN _____

NOUN _____

CELEBRITY _____

VERB ENDING IN "ING" _____

ADJECTIVE _____

YOUR NAME _____

ADJECTIVE _____

A PLACE _____

PLURAL NOUN _____

ADJECTIVE _____

VERB ENDING IN "ING" _____

PERSON YOU KNOW _____

VERB ENDING IN "ING" _____

ADJECTIVE _____

YOUR NAME _____

ADVERB _____

VERB ENDING IN "ING" _____

MAD LIBS

WHO TOOTED?

Rehearsal for the _____ Day parade was not going well.

PLURAL NOUN

Our bass drum player kept dropping his sticks, first-_____

NOUN

tuba _____ had her sheet music upside down, and the

CELEBRITY

flutist was _____ louder than the entire band! Then,

VERB ENDING IN "ING"

just when we thought it couldn't get worse, something _____

ADJECTIVE

happened during _____'s solo. The most _____

YOUR NAME   ADJECTIVE

smell drifted through (the) _____. It smelled like baked

A PLACE

_____ and _____ dogs . . . The _____

PLURAL NOUN   ADJECTIVE   VERB ENDING IN "ING"

Band Tooter was back! But who was it? Could it be _____,

PERSON YOU KNOW

on the bass drum? Was he _____ gas to get out of

VERB ENDING IN "ING"

practice? Or was it the first-chair tuba? Band was a/an _____

ADJECTIVE

joke to her, and farts were hilarious. Or was it _____,

YOUR NAME

the flutist? Everyone knew that she really wanted the piccolo solo. But

just *how* _____ did she want it? Enough to be the

ADVERB

_____ Band Tooter? You decide.

VERB ENDING IN "ING"

MAD LIBS® is fun to play with friends, but you can also play it by yourself! To begin with, DO NOT look at the story on the page below. Fill in the blanks on this page with the words called for. Then, using the words you have selected, fill in the blank spaces in the story.

Now you've created your own hilarious MAD LIBS® game!

RECIPE FOR DISASTER

TYPE OF FOOD _____

NUMBER _____

OCCUPATION _____

YOUR NAME _____

TYPE OF LIQUID _____

NOUN _____

ADJECTIVE _____

NUMBER _____

ADVERB _____

PLURAL NOUN _____

TYPE OF FOOD (PLURAL) _____

ADJECTIVE _____

VERB _____

TYPE OF CONTAINER _____

TYPE OF LIQUID _____

ADJECTIVE _____

SILLY WORD _____

NOUN _____

MAD LIBS®

RECIPE FOR DISASTER

For the grossest _____ of your life, enjoy this recipe from
                        TYPE OF FOOD

_____-star _____ _____:
NUMBER   OCCUPATION   YOUR NAME

• Combine fresh _____ with two scoops of _____
                 TYPE OF LIQUID   NOUN

powder and whisk till chunky.

• Once _____, pour in _____ gallons of mayonnaise
       ADJECTIVE   NUMBER

to thicken.

• _____ fold in six pickled _____ and the zest
  ADVERB   PLURAL NOUN

of two _____.
       TYPE OF FOOD (PLURAL)

• With a/an _____ spoon, _____ the mixture into
           ADJECTIVE   VERB

a large _____ and place on a stove.
        TYPE OF CONTAINER

• Bring the _____ to a/an _____ boil and
            TYPE OF LIQUID   ADJECTIVE

immediately place in the freezer to cool.

• Once frozen, garnish with chopped _____ onions,
                                    SILLY WORD

_____-melon puree, and bacon bits to serve!
NOUN

MAD LIBS® is fun to play with friends, but you can also play it by yourself! To begin with, DO NOT look at the story on the page below. Fill in the blanks on this page with the words called for. Then, using the words you have selected, fill in the blank spaces in the story.

Now you've created your own hilarious MAD LIBS® game!

SKUNK'S STORY

SILLY WORD _____

ADJECTIVE _____

LAST NAME _____

VERB ENDING IN "ING" _____

COLOR _____

COLOR _____

VERB _____

PART OF THE BODY _____

PART OF THE BODY _____

EXCLAMATION _____

ADJECTIVE _____

SOMETHING ALIVE (PLURAL) _____

ANIMAL (PLURAL) _____

PLURAL NOUN _____

ADJECTIVE _____

VERB _____

ADJECTIVE _____

PLURAL NOUN _____

MAD LIBS®

SKUNK'S STORY

Hi, _____ the skunk here, with a story about how I tried to
     SILLY WORD

meet some _____ humans at Old Mc-_____'s farm.
      ADJECTIVE   LAST NAME

The farmers first saw me when I was out _____ their
                                    VERB ENDING IN "ING"

flowers. To show them how nice I am, I waved my _____ -and-
                                      COLOR

_____ bushy tail in the air. I knew the humans would
     COLOR

_____ it, because my tail stands out like a sore _____.
  VERB   PART OF THE BODY

Then, I batted my _____-lashes and tried my best to look
               PART OF THE BODY

adorable. But then one of the humans shouted, "_____! Skunk!
                                  EXCLAMATION

Run!" And just like that, I was left alone again. How _____!
                                    ADJECTIVE

Humans don't run away from kittens, fuzzy _____,
                        SOMETHING ALIVE (PLURAL)

bunnies, or _____, so why do they run away from skunks?
          ANIMAL (PLURAL)

Sure, we spray smelly _____ when we're _____,
                PLURAL NOUN   ADJECTIVE

but it's only self-defense! We usually smell quite lovely! I _____
                                      VERB

my fur and take _____, long baths daily. Do dogs do that? No
           ADJECTIVE

way! But human _____ love dogs. Why? Who knows!
          PLURAL NOUN

MAD LIBS® is fun to play with friends, but you can also play it by yourself! To begin with, DO NOT look at the story on the page below. Fill in the blanks on this page with the words called for. Then, using the words you have selected, fill in the blank spaces in the story.

Now you've created your own hilarious MAD LIBS® game!

ZOMBIE SPA

VERB _____

NOUN _____

PART OF THE BODY (PLURAL) _____

ADJECTIVE _____

TYPE OF FOOD _____

CITY _____

NUMBER _____

NOUN _____

ADJECTIVE _____

SAME NOUN _____

TYPE OF LIQUID _____

NUMBER _____

SOMETHING ALIVE _____

ADJECTIVE _____

PART OF THE BODY (PLURAL) _____

ANIMAL _____

NUMBER _____

VERB _____

MAD LIBS®

ZOMBIE SPA

Why smell like a rose when you can _____ like a/an _____?

VERB   NOUN

Choose from any of the Zombie Spa services below to keep your

_____ feeling slimy and _____:

PART OF THE BODY (PLURAL)   ADJECTIVE

- **Compost Facial:** Banana peels, _____ -shells, and

TYPE OF FOOD

  _____'s finest soil create a facial that will leave you looking

CITY

  _____ years old.

NUMBER

- **Deluxe _____ Bath:** Sink into our signature _____

NOUN   ADJECTIVE

  _____ bath where the _____ is heated to a

SAME NOUN   TYPE OF LIQUID

  perfect _____ degrees. _____ added on request.

NUMBER   SOMETHING ALIVE

- **The Million-Fish Kiss:** Are your feet _____ and tired?

ADJECTIVE

  Give those bunions a rest and dip your _____

PART OF THE BODY (PLURAL)

  into our soothing _____ tank, where _____ tiny

ANIMAL   NUMBER

  fish will _____ your dead skin with kisses! Delightful!

VERB

MAD LIBS® is fun to play with friends, but you can also play it by yourself! To begin with, DO NOT look at the story on the page below. Fill in the blanks on this page with the words called for. Then, using the words you have selected, fill in the blank spaces in the story.

Now you've created your own hilarious MAD LIBS® game!

ARE YOU GONNA EAT THAT?

NOUN _____

SAME NOUN _____

VERB _____

NOUN _____

PERSON YOU KNOW _____

PLURAL NOUN _____

EXCLAMATION _____

PART OF THE BODY _____

NOUN _____

ADJECTIVE _____

ADJECTIVE _____

SILLY WORD _____

NOUN _____

VERB _____

ANIMAL (PLURAL) _____

TYPE OF FOOD _____

VERB ENDING IN "ING" _____

ADJECTIVE _____

MAD LIBS

ARE YOU GONNA EAT THAT?

The best part of having a/an _____-day party is eating the
                                    NOUN

_____-day cake. I can't wait to _____ a slice! Ooh!
    SAME NOUN   VERB

The birthday _____, _____, is getting ready to
                    NOUN   PERSON YOU KNOW

blow out the _____. They're making a wish and . . .
                    PLURAL NOUN

_____! It's time to cut the cake. I have my _____
    EXCLAMATION   PART OF THE BODY

on a corner slice—it's got the best frosting-to- _____ ratio
                                                        NOUN

and rainbow sprinkles. Before anyone else can see my slice, I swipe it

from the table. It's just as _____ as I thought it would be.
                                ADJECTIVE

Spongy and creamy and _____ and . . . oh my _____.
                            ADJECTIVE   SILLY WORD

What's that? Is that a/an _____ fly? *In* my cake? Do I spit
                                NOUN

it out, do I scream, do I _____? What do I do?
                                VERB

What if there were other _____ in my slice . . . and I ate
                            ANIMAL (PLURAL)

them, too? But on the flip side, the _____ is so delicious.
                                        TYPE OF FOOD

Should I keep _____ it? After all, it was just a/an
                VERB ENDING IN "ING"

_____ bug!
    ADJECTIVE

MAD LIBS® is fun to play with friends, but you can also play it by yourself! To begin with, DO NOT look at the story on the page below. Fill in the blanks on this page with the words called for. Then, using the words you have selected, fill in the blank spaces in the story.

Now you've created your own hilarious MAD LIBS® game!

TOILET: TRUE OR FALSE?

VERB _____

NOUN _____

OCCUPATION _____

SOMETHING ALIVE (PLURAL) _____

ADJECTIVE _____

TYPE OF CONTAINER _____

VERB _____

NOUN _____

NOUN _____

A PLACE _____

NUMBER _____

PLURAL NOUN _____

PART OF THE BODY (PLURAL) _____

PLURAL NOUN _____

ADVERB _____

VERB _____

MAD LIBS®

TOILET: TRUE OR FALSE?

Answer these questions correctly to _____ your spot on the
_____VERB_____

porcelain _____ as the "_____ of Toilet Trivia":
_____NOUN_____   _____OCCUPATION_____

1. Your kitchen sink has more microscopic _____
_____SOMETHING ALIVE (PLURAL)_____

   than a/an _____ toilet _____. (T or F)
   _____ADJECTIVE_____   _____TYPE OF CONTAINER_____

2. You _____ confetti and bake a/an _____ to
   _____VERB_____   _____NOUN_____

   celebrate World Toilet Day every November. (T or F)

3. The average _____ uses (the) _____ twenty-five
   _____NOUN_____   _____A PLACE_____

   hundred times in a year. (T or F)

4. Only _____ percent of _____ wash their
   _____NUMBER_____   _____PLURAL NOUN_____

   _____ after using the toilet. (T or F)
   _____PART OF THE BODY (PLURAL)_____

If you answered True for all the _____ . . . you
                                  _____PLURAL NOUN_____

_____ know your stuff! Now go _____ your hands!
_____ADVERB_____   _____VERB_____

MAD LIBS® is fun to play with friends, but you can also play it by yourself! To begin with, DO NOT look at the story on the page below. Fill in the blanks on this page with the words called for. Then, using the words you have selected, fill in the blank spaces in the story.

Now you've created your own hilarious MAD LIBS® game!

VERY MESSY ROOM

YOUR NAME _____

NOUN _____

COUNTRY _____

PLURAL NOUN _____

NUMBER _____

ARTICLE OF CLOTHING (PLURAL) _____

ADJECTIVE _____

ADJECTIVE _____

PLURAL NOUN _____

NOUN _____

ANIMAL _____

TYPE OF FOOD _____

ANIMAL _____

SAME ANIMAL (PLURAL) _____

TYPE OF LIQUID _____

ADJECTIVE _____

ARTICLE OF CLOTHING (PLURAL) _____

ADJECTIVE _____

MAD LIBS®

VERY MESSY ROOM

Hi! I'm Sloppy _____ and I have the messiest _____
        YOUR NAME   NOUN

in all of _____! Come on in, and I'll give you a tour! First, we
        COUNTRY

have my leaning tower of _____. This pile is _____
                          PLURAL NOUN   NUMBER

feet tall and is made from old _____. In fact,
                                ARTICLE OF CLOTHING (PLURAL)

it's the tallest tower of unwashed clothes on the _____ coast!
                                                   ADJECTIVE

Pretty impressive, huh? Speaking of _____, this heap of
                                      ADJECTIVE

_____ has been covering my bed for months. If you get
    PLURAL NOUN

close, you can smell my _____-sheets. They smell like wet
                            NOUN

_____, _____ jerky, and a touch of relish. Oh! And
    ANIMAL   TYPE OF FOOD

I almost forgot to show you my _____ tank! There's no real
                                  ANIMAL

_____ in it, but it's filled with _____ and
SAME ANIMAL (PLURAL)   TYPE OF LIQUID

has got _____ algae growing on the glass. Just the way I like
          ADJECTIVE

it. Wait a minute. Where'd you go? Uh-oh. I think I lost you back in

the _____ tower. I told you this place was
      ARTICLE OF CLOTHING (PLURAL)

_____!
    ADJECTIVE

MAD LIBS® is fun to play with friends, but you can also play it by yourself! To begin with, DO NOT look at the story on the page below. Fill in the blanks on this page with the words called for. Then, using the words you have selected, fill in the blank spaces in the story.

Now you've created your own hilarious MAD LIBS® game!

FREAKY FUNKY FASHION

PERSON YOU KNOW _____

COLOR _____

COUNTRY _____

OCCUPATION (PLURAL) _____

ARTICLE OF CLOTHING (PLURAL) _____

PART OF THE BODY _____

COLOR _____

ADJECTIVE _____

VERB _____

EXCLAMATION _____

LETTER OF THE ALPHABET _____

PLURAL NOUN _____

TYPE OF FOOD _____

VEHICLE _____

VERB ENDING IN "ING" _____

NUMBER _____

NOUN _____

ADJECTIVE _____

MAD LIBS®

FREAKY FUNKY FASHION

Hi, I'm _____, reporting live from the _____
      PERSON YOU KNOW   COLOR

carpet at this year's Yuck Awards— _____'s ugliest night in
                                   COUNTRY

fashion. _____ and fashion designers from around the
          OCCUPATION (PLURAL)

globe have joined together to knock your _____
                              ARTICLE OF CLOTHING (PLURAL)

off with their _____-dropping creations. Here comes our
          PART OF THE BODY

first celebrity—it's Henrietta _____! Her gown is inspired by
                      COLOR

a/an _____ sardine tin, and she completes her look with a/an
      ADJECTIVE

_____-and-sniff purse. Let's give it a try . . . _____!
      VERB   EXCLAMATION

It really stinks! Next is _____-list celebrity Jay
                     LETTER OF THE ALPHABET

_____, sporting a tuxedo made of used dental floss. If you
    PLURAL NOUN

look closely, you can see bits of _____ stuck to the floss. And
                       TYPE OF FOOD

now, a garbage _____ has arrived and is _____
            VEHICLE   VERB ENDING IN "ING"

_____ tons of trash onto the red carpet. The _____
  NUMBER   NOUN

Brothers are emerging from the waste! Can this night get any more

_____? Stick with us to find out!
  ADJECTIVE

MAD LIBS® is fun to play with friends, but you can also play it by yourself! To begin with, DO NOT look at the story on the page below. Fill in the blanks on this page with the words called for. Then, using the words you have selected, fill in the blank spaces in the story.

Now you've created your own hilarious MAD LIBS® game!

HANDKERCHIEF DEBATE

ADJECTIVE _____

NUMBER _____

PLURAL NOUN _____

NUMBER _____

PLURAL NOUN _____

TYPE OF BUILDING _____

PART OF THE BODY _____

VERB _____

PLURAL NOUN _____

A PLACE _____

NUMBER _____

VERB _____

ADJECTIVE _____

NUMBER _____

VEHICLE (PLURAL) _____

VERB ENDING IN "ING" _____

ADJECTIVE _____

PART OF THE BODY (PLURAL) _____

MAD LIBS®

HANDKERCHIEF DEBATE

Are handkerchiefs useful or _____? We polled over _____

ADJECTIVE
NUMBER

_____ and the results are in. Which side are you on?

PLURAL NOUN

- **Pro-handkerchief:** _____ percent of _____ are

NUMBER
PLURAL NOUN

  pro-hanky. And not just the folks in the nursing _____,

TYPE OF BUILDING

  either! _____-kerchiefs may be an invention from the

PART OF THE BODY

  past, but they can _____ the future! Who knew having a

VERB

  rag in your pocket that's covered in green _____ can

PLURAL NOUN

  help save (the) _____!

A PLACE

- **Anti-handkerchief:** _____ percent of people are anti-hanky!

NUMBER

  Don't _____ germs with a/an _____, used

VERB
ADJECTIVE

  cloth tissue. Is this the year 18-_____? We have self-driving

NUMBER

  _____, delivery drones, and _____

VEHICLE (PLURAL)
VERB ENDING IN "ING"

  robots now. Why would we reuse a/an _____ cloth to

ADJECTIVE

  blow our _____?

PART OF THE BODY (PLURAL)

MAD LIBS® is fun to play with friends, but you can also play it by yourself! To begin with, DO NOT look at the story on the page below. Fill in the blanks on this page with the words called for. Then, using the words you have selected, fill in the blank spaces in the story.

Now you've created your own hilarious MAD LIBS® game!

THE LEGEND OF BATHROOM STALL THREE

TYPE OF BUILDING _____

NUMBER _____

VERB ENDING IN "ING" _____

ARTICLE OF CLOTHING (PLURAL) _____

NOUN _____

ANIMAL (PLURAL) _____

VERB _____

VERB ENDING IN "S" _____

CELEBRITY _____

TYPE OF LIQUID _____

EXCLAMATION _____

NOUN _____

ADJECTIVE _____

PLURAL NOUN _____

YOUR NAME _____

VERB (PAST TENSE) _____

NOUN _____

MAD LIBS®
THE LEGEND OF
BATHROOM STALL THREE

Hey, new kid! If you learn anything on your first day of middle

_____, let it be this: Beware of Stall Three.
TYPE OF BUILDING

- Never in _____ years, even if it's an emergency, use Stall
  NUMBER

  Three. _____ in your _____
  VERB ENDING IN "ING"   ARTICLE OF CLOTHING (PLURAL)

  is the better option.

- There's a ghost _____ that's been floating in that haunted
  NOUN

  toilet since the _____ roamed the earth. Don't let it
  ANIMAL (PLURAL)

  _____ you!
  VERB

- That toilet _____ water on you if you flush it.
  VERB ENDING IN "S"

  _____ went in there once, and then they smelled like
  CELEBRITY

  _____ for a year. _____!
  TYPE OF LIQUID   EXCLAMATION

- The _____ seat is extremely _____ and can
  NOUN   ADJECTIVE

  trap you there for hours, days, or even _____!
  PLURAL NOUN

  _____ was a first grader when they _____
  YOUR NAME   VERB (PAST TENSE)

  down on that sticky _____, and they were stuck there until
  NOUN

  the eighth grade!

MAD LIBS® is fun to play with friends, but you can also play it by yourself! To begin with, DO NOT look at the story on the page below. Fill in the blanks on this page with the words called for. Then, using the words you have selected, fill in the blank spaces in the story.

Now you've created your own hilarious MAD LIBS® game!

ICKY ANIMALS

ADJECTIVE _____

COLOR _____

SILLY WORD _____

VERB ENDING IN "ING" _____

PART OF THE BODY (PLURAL) _____

NUMBER _____

ANIMAL _____

COLOR _____

PART OF THE BODY (PLURAL) _____

ADJECTIVE _____

COLOR _____

ADJECTIVE _____

NUMBER _____

VERB _____

SILLY WORD _____

SAME SILLY WORD _____

ADVERB _____

MAD LIBS

ICKY ANIMALS

Some animals are so cute and _____ they make you want to
                          ADJECTIVE
say, "Awwww!" But these animals do not:

• _____-faced _____ monkeys say hello by
        COLOR   SILLY WORD
_____ their friend's _____.
VERB ENDING IN "ING"   PART OF THE BODY (PLURAL)

• _____-toed sloths are often covered in algae and _____
     NUMBER   ANIMAL
eggs, turning their fur a slimy _____ hue.
                                 COLOR

• After shedding their _____, lots of frogs, like
                        PART OF THE BODY (PLURAL)
the African _____ frog, eat their dead skin.
             ADJECTIVE

• When a/an _____ whale farts, they create a bubble in the
              COLOR
ocean that's _____ enough to fit a horse inside it!
              ADJECTIVE

• In only _____ hours, an elephant can _____ a piece
           NUMBER   VERB
of _____ _____ that weighs as much as a/an
   SILLY WORD   SAME SILLY WORD
_____ grown human.
 ADVERB

MAD LIBS® is fun to play with friends, but you can also play it by yourself! To begin with, DO NOT look at the story on the page below. Fill in the blanks on this page with the words called for. Then, using the words you have selected, fill in the blank spaces in the story.

Now you've created your own hilarious MAD LIBS® game!

MEAT LOAF MADNESS

ADJECTIVE _____

TYPE OF FOOD _____

OCCUPATION _____

LAST NAME _____

ADJECTIVE _____

ADJECTIVE _____

VERB _____

NOUN _____

OCCUPATION _____

SOMETHING ALIVE _____

SAME TYPE OF FOOD _____

VERB ENDING IN "ING" _____

PART OF THE BODY (PLURAL) _____

LAST NAME _____

PLURAL NOUN _____

TYPE OF BUILDING _____

SAME TYPE OF FOOD _____

MAD LIBS®

MEAT LOAF MADNESS

As if Mondays weren't _____ enough, our school cafeteria starts
                        ADJECTIVE

each week by serving _____ loaf. It's made with our
                          TYPE OF FOOD

_____ Mrs. _____'s secret recipe. The recipe is
   OCCUPATION   LAST NAME

so secret, even she doesn't know what's in it! Some days the meat loaf is

_____, some days it's sour, and some days it's so _____,
   ADJECTIVE   ADJECTIVE

it bounces! Once I saw it _____ in the dark. But this week . . .
                              VERB

it was alive! At first, when we heard the _____ alarm go off,
                                              NOUN

we thought it was an ordinary drill. But when our school _____
                                                            OCCUPATION

started crying for his _____ over the loudspeaker, we knew
                       SOMETHING ALIVE

we were in trouble! The _____ loaf was mutating! It
                          SAME TYPE OF FOOD

started _____ arms and _____!
        VERB ENDING IN "ING"   PART OF THE BODY (PLURAL)

Mrs. _____ tried to fight it off with mustard, spatulas,
       LAST NAME

_____, and even fire . . . but nothing worked! She had
   PLURAL NOUN

created a monster! Our _____ was under attack, but hey, at
                        TYPE OF BUILDING

least we didn't have to eat that _____ loaf!
                                 SAME TYPE OF FOOD

MAD LIBS® is fun to play with friends, but you can also play it by yourself! To begin with, DO NOT look at the story on the page below. Fill in the blanks on this page with the words called for. Then, using the words you have selected, fill in the blank spaces in the story.

Now you've created your own hilarious MAD LIBS® game!

PUTRID PARTY PLANNING

NOUN _____

VERB _____

TYPE OF EVENT _____

VERB _____

ADJECTIVE _____

ANIMAL (PLURAL) _____

ADJECTIVE _____

PART OF THE BODY (PLURAL) _____

TYPE OF CONTAINER _____

ADJECTIVE _____

PLURAL NOUN _____

COLOR _____

VERB _____

PLURAL NOUN _____

VERB ENDING IN "ING" _____

PART OF THE BODY (PLURAL) _____

ADJECTIVE _____

EXCLAMATION _____

MAD LIBS®

PUTRID PARTY PLANNING

Tired of hosting fancy _____ parties or boring _____-overs?
                        NOUN   VERB

Throw a gross-out _____ instead with these icky tips:
                   TYPE OF EVENT

- Don't just _____ any kind of dinner. Make it _____!
             VERB   ADJECTIVE

  Cut up ten meatless hot _____ and add ketchup to
                          ANIMAL (PLURAL)

  make them look like _____ _____!
                      ADJECTIVE   PART OF THE BODY (PLURAL)

  Creepy!

- When decorating, think outside the _____. Hang
                                     TYPE OF CONTAINER

  _____ toilet paper on the _____ instead of
  ADJECTIVE   PLURAL NOUN

  streamers and balloons! Use _____ slime to make your
                              COLOR

  guests _____!
         VERB

- Don't forget games! Blindfold your party _____
                                           PLURAL NOUN

  and trick them into thinking they're _____
                                       VERB ENDING IN "ING"

  slimy _____. Cold spaghetti can feel
        PART OF THE BODY (PLURAL)

  like _____ brains! _____!
       ADJECTIVE   EXCLAMATION

MAD LIBS® is fun to play with friends, but you can also play it by yourself! To begin with, DO NOT look at the story on the page below. Fill in the blanks on this page with the words called for. Then, using the words you have selected, fill in the blank spaces in the story.

Now you've created your own hilarious MAD LIBS® game!

POEM BY A CAT

NOUN _____

ADJECTIVE _____

PART OF THE BODY _____

ADVERB _____

ANIMAL (PLURAL) _____

NOUN _____

TYPE OF BUILDING _____

ADJECTIVE _____

ADJECTIVE _____

VERB _____

ANIMAL (PLURAL) _____

VERB _____

NOUN _____

NOUN _____

ADJECTIVE _____

MAD LIBS®

POEM BY A CAT

Hairball, _____-ball, I hate you.
NOUN

You're _____ and gross, and that is true.
ADJECTIVE

You hurt my _____ and smell _____ bad.
PART OF THE BODY   ADVERB

You make _____ everywhere sad.
ANIMAL (PLURAL)

If you were a/an _____, I'd scratch your face.
NOUN

If I went to your _____, I'd wreck the place.
TYPE OF BUILDING

You're _____ and sticky. And _____, too.
ADJECTIVE   ADJECTIVE

Did I mention how much I hate you?

I _____ you more than _____ and dogs.
VERB   ANIMAL (PLURAL)

I _____ you more than litter-box hogs.
VERB

You're my least favorite thing about being a cat.

I would rather share my _____ with a rat.
NOUN

Hairball, _____-ball, I hate you.
NOUN

You're _____ and gross, and that is true!
ADJECTIVE

MAD LIBS® is fun to play with friends, but you can also play it by yourself! To begin with, DO NOT look at the story on the page below. Fill in the blanks on this page with the words called for. Then, using the words you have selected, fill in the blank spaces in the story.

Now you've created your own hilarious MAD LIBS® game!

STINK MASTER 3000

SOMETHING ALIVE (PLURAL) _____

SILLY WORD _____

VERB _____

NOUN _____

OCCUPATION _____

NOUN _____

NOUN _____

NUMBER _____

ADJECTIVE _____

PART OF THE BODY _____

TYPE OF BUILDING _____

ADJECTIVE _____

TYPE OF CONTAINER _____

TYPE OF EVENT _____

VERB ENDING IN "S" _____

SAME TYPE OF CONTAINER _____

VERB ENDING IN "ING" _____

MAD LIBS®

STINK MASTER 3000

Tired of pranking your best _____ with the same
SOMETHING ALIVE (PLURAL)

old _____ cushion gag? Wish you could make them _____
SILLY WORD VERB

without spending hundreds of dollars? Well, now you can! With the

_____ Master 3000, you can become the _____ of
NOUN OCCUPATION

your dreams. It's so easy to use, a/an _____ could do it! This
NOUN

state-of-the-art _____ blaster comes preloaded with _____
NOUN NUMBER

stinky scents. From _____ egg breath to _____
ADJECTIVE PART OF THE BODY

sweat, stink up an entire _____ with the press of a button.
TYPE OF BUILDING

And all this can be yours for the _____ price of $19.95. And
ADJECTIVE

for a limited time, we're throwing in a custom _____ to trap
TYPE OF CONTAINER

and store your favorite scents for up to five days. Can't make it to your

aunt's _____ but still want to prank her as she _____
TYPE OF EVENT VERB ENDING IN "S"

down the aisle? Simply use the _____ to trap
SAME TYPE OF CONTAINER

the smell and ship it through the mail! It's that easy! So, what are you

_____ for? Call today!
VERB ENDING IN "ING"

MAD LIBS® is fun to play with friends, but you can also play it by yourself! To begin with, DO NOT look at the story on the page below. Fill in the blanks on this page with the words called for. Then, using the words you have selected, fill in the blank spaces in the story.

Now you've created your own hilarious MAD LIBS® game!

HOW GROSS ARE YOU?

ADJECTIVE _____

VERB ENDING IN "ING" _____

A PLACE _____

NUMBER _____

VERB _____

PART OF THE BODY _____

PLURAL NOUN _____

NUMBER _____

VERB ENDING IN "ING" _____

VERB _____

TYPE OF CONTAINER _____

PART OF THE BODY _____

NOUN _____

PLURAL NOUN _____

OCCUPATION _____

MAD LIBS®

HOW GROSS ARE YOU?

How _____ are you? Tally up your score on our Mad Libs
      ADJECTIVE

Gross-O-Meter to find out! Do you . . .

- Go to sleep without _____ your teeth? (1 point)
        VERB ENDING IN "ING"

- Sniff your sweaty _____ socks to see if you can wear them
        A PLACE

  _____ more times? (2 points)
      NUMBER

- Check your tissue after you _____ your _____
        VERB   PART OF THE BODY

  to see what color your _____ are? (3 points)
        PLURAL NOUN

- Always make sure to follow the _____-_minute_ rule when it
        NUMBER

  comes to _____ food off the floor? (4 points)
      VERB ENDING IN "ING"

- _____ your scabs . . . and flick them in the _____?
    VERB   TYPE OF CONTAINER

  (5 points)

- Clip your _____-nails at the _____ table?
      PART OF THE BODY   NOUN

  (6 points)

Gross-O-Meter Score Key:

0–5 points: Not gross enough!

6–10 _____: Super gross!
    PLURAL NOUN

11–21 points: See a/an _____!
      OCCUPATION